Afterwards

Janet Moran

T0284203

methuen | drama

LONDON • NEW YORK • OXFORD • NEW DELHI • SYDNEY

METHUEN DRAMA
Bloomsbury Publishing Plc
50 Bedford Square, London, WC1B 3DP, UK
1385 Broadway, New York, NY 10018, USA
29 Earlsfort Terrace, Dublin 2, Ireland

BLOOMSBURY, METHUEN DRAMA and the Methuen
Drama logo are trademarks of Bloomsbury Publishing Plc

First published in Great Britain 2024

Cover design: Neil O'Driscoll

ISBN: PB: 978-1-3505-2908-3
ePDF: 978-1-3505-2909-0
eBook: 978-1-3505-2910-6

Series: Modern Plays

Typeset by Mark Heslington Ltd, Scarborough, North Yorkshire
Printed and bound in Great Britain

To find out more about our authors and books visit
www.bloomsbury.com and sign up for our newsletters.

Once Off Productions presents

Afterwards

by Janet Moran

directed by Conall Morrison and Janet Moran

co-presented by The Abbey Theatre and Dublin
Fringe Festival

Cast

Cork Woman	Kate Stanley Brennan
English Woman	Sophie Lenglinger
Young Woman	Ebby O'Toole-Acheampong
Orderly	Shadaan Felfeli
Young Man	David Rawle
Voice of Doctor	Shane O'Reilly

Creative Team

Writer & Co-Director	Janet Moran
Director	Conall Morrison
Set & Costume Designer	LaurA Fajardo Castro
Lighting Designer	Suzie Cummins
Composer & Sound Designer	Denis Clohessy
AV Designer	Neil O'Driscoll
Dramaturg	Jessica Traynor
Assistant Director	Friederike Karpf
Hair & Make-Up	Tee Elliott

Production Team

Producer	Cally Shine
Production Manager	Veronica Foo
Stage Manager	Zoë Reynolds
Company Manager	Morgan Steele
Assistant Stage Manager	Sarah Purcell
Costume Supervisors	Dara Gill & Maisey Lorimer
Chief LX	Ross McSherry
LX Programmer	Maeubh Brennan
Promotional Artwork	Neil O'Driscoll
Production Photography	Patricio Cassinoni

For Once Off Productions

Director	Maura O'Keeffe
Senior Producer	Orla Flanagan
Finance Officer	Catherine Finn
Associate Producer	Sadhbh Barrett Coakley

Associate Producer	Cally Shine
Company Manager	Morgan Steele
Assistant Producer	Sinéad Gallagher
Assistant Producer	Miles Harrigan
Marketing Associate	Ciara Gogarty

This production runs for approximately 90 minutes, with no interval.

Afterwards was first performed on the Peacock Stage, Abbey Theatre, Dublin, on 9 September 2024 (previews from 6 September), before transferring to the Mermaid Arts Centre, Bray, Co. Wicklow, on 18 September 2024. The premiere production was supported by Fishamble's New Play Clinic, and funded by the Arts Council of Ireland/An Chomhairle Ealaíon.

Janet Moran is an actor and playwright based in Dublin. She has performed at the Abbey Theatre, The Gate Theatre, Dublin, the National Theatre UK as well as with many other Irish and UK companies and on stages in the US, France, Mexico and New Zealand. In 2023, she received the Irish Times Best Actress Award. She co-wrote and performed in the hit play *Swing* which toured both nationally and internationally between 2013 and 2016. *Swing* was published by Bloomsbury Press in 2015. She wrote and directed *A Holy Show* which played a sell-out run at the Peacock Theatre as part of Dublin Fringe before transferring to Edinburgh Fringe, CCI Paris and completing a sold out national tour in 2019. *A Holy Show* was subsequently adapted for RTE Drama on One. In 2020, she co-wrote and directed *Pure Mental* (national tour and First Fortnight Festival) and *Looking for América* which played at the Mermaid Arts Centre as part of Dublin Theatre Festival and Assembly at Edinburgh Fringe. *Looking for América* was chosen by Screen Ireland to be developed into a screenplay as part of their Spotlight programme. In 2023 her play *Quake* premiered as part of Dublin Theatre Festival at the Samuel Beckett Theatre and was named one of the top fifty shows in the UK and Ireland by The Stage UK. *Quake* was also nominated for a Writers Guild of Ireland (Zebbie) Award in 2024.

Conall Morrison is a director and playwright. As well as directing twenty plays for the Abbey and Peacock theatres, he has directed for the Royal Shakespeare Company, Royal National Theatre, the Globe Theatre, English National Opera, Irish National Opera, Landmark Productions, Blue Raincoat, Fishamble: The New Play Company, the Lyric Theatre, Cameron Mackintosh Productions. As well as several original plays, he has done many adaptations, including *Woyzeck in Winter*, *Tarry Flynn*, *Antigone*, *Ghosts*, *The Travels of Jonathan Swift*. He has directed six RTE radio dramas, most recently *Helen's Wheels* by Fionn Foley. Previous productions for Once Off include: *The United States vs Ulysses* by Colin Murphy and *Quake* by Janet Moran. He recently directed Billy Roche's *A Handful of Stars* for Four Rivers Theatre Company.

Kate Stanley Brennan is an award-winning performer/creative from Dublin. For twenty years, she has worked extensively in theatre across Ireland and internationally including: US/UK/Irish tour *The Plough and the Stars* (Abbey Theatre); *White Devil* (Shakespeare's Globe, Dublin/Australian tour); *Terminus* (NYC/Irish tour); *Conversations After Sex* (world tour); *Riot* (ThisIsPopBaby). Film work includes: *Twig* (Blue Ink); *KIN* (Townsend Film/AMC); *FloatLike a Butterfly* (Samson); *DollHouse* (winner of Best Ensemble Odessa Film Fest, Visit Films). Her writer/director credits include: *Panto* (Screen Ireland's Actor as Creator winner Best Film, Women in Film and Television awards, IFI and Best Short, Feedback Female FF L.A.); *Cherry* (Best Short nomination, Chicago Irish FF); *Walk For Me* (ProjectArtsCentre/ShowInABag). She writes/releases music under MissKate.

Sophie Lenglinger graduated from the Lir National Academy of Dramatic Art in Dublin in 2022. She is the female lead in the Paramount+ miniseries *Stags*, Sophie's screen debut. She will play the role of Brett in the feature *Whitetail*, directed by Nanouk Leopold. Upon graduating from Lir, Sophie was cast as Nora in the Druid production of *The Plough and the Stars*, as part of *DruidO'Casey*: Seán O'Casey's Dublin Trilogy. The production toured Ireland and was performed at the Abbey Theatre in Dublin, followed by a run in New York. Previous work with Once Off Productions Includes: world premiere of *Absent the Wrong* by Carys D. Coburn.

Ebby O'Toole-Acheampong is an actress from Dublin who graduated from the Lir Academy in 2023. Ebby's theatre credits include: *The Quare Fellow* (Abbey Theatre) and *Hothouse* (Malaprop Theatre). TV credits include: *The School*

Trip (Channel 5); *Moonflower Murders* (BBC); *Into the Badlands* (AMC) and *Redwater* (BBC).

Shadaan Felfeli has an MA in Drama and Performance Studies from UCD and has trained at the Gaiety School of Acting, Dublin. Theatre credits include: *The Treaty* (Fishamble/National Concert Hall/Embassy of Ireland, London); *Home Theatre [Ireland]* (Dublin Theatre Festival/Draoícht); *My Name is Language* (Dublin Theatre Festival/Project Arts Centre); *The Other War* (Festabit/Project Arts Centre); *Waiting for Godot* (Mouth on Fire Theatre Co./Theatre X Cai, Tokyo/Kyoto University of Arts & Design); *One for the Road* (Gate Theatre); *A Midsummer Night's Dream* (Abbey Theatre); *Rough for Theatre II, Catastrophe* (Mouth on Fire Theatre Co./National Concert Hall); *The Burning House* (Dublin Dance Festival); *Bodach an Chóta Lachna* (Baboró Children's Festival, national tour).

David Rawle is an actor from Leitrim based in Dublin. He graduated from the Lir Academy in 2022. David can be seen in Chris O' Dowd's new comedy drama *Small Town Big Story* for Sky TV, released in 2024. He played the role of Alan in *Falling for the Life of Alex Whelan*, the RTÉ Storyland short directed and written by Nell Hensey. On stage, David played Dan in Livin Dred's production of *Danti-Dan* directed by Aaron Monaghan, which toured Ireland in 2023. He played the role of Declan in *The Blackwater Lightship* based on the book by Colm Tóibín, directed and adapted by David Horan as part of the Dublin Theatre Festival 2022. Film and TV work includes: Martin Moone in *Moone Boy*, Ben in Cartoon Saloon's *Song of the Sea*, Brendan O' Donnell in *Property of the State*, Dermot in *Drop Dead Weird, Pixie*.

LaurA Fajardo Castro is a Colombian costume and set designer based in Dublin. She has worked for theatre, dance, opera and TV. LaurA graduated with a Bachelor in Fine Arts from Los Andes University in Bogotá, Colombia. In 2019 she graduated with an MFA in Stage Design from the

Lir Academy, Trinity College Dublin. Her recent design works include: *ÍOMHÁ* by Róisín Whelan Dance Company at the Carlow Arts Festival; *The Ireland We Dreamed Of* by Sinead McCann; *You Belong To Me* by Rory Nolan for Once Off Productions, Rough Magic and Smock Alley Theatre; *The Visit, Bulrusher* and *Three Sisters* at the Lir Academy; *Fall and Float* by Mónica Muñoz Dance and more. In Bogotá, LaurA worked for four years with the theatre company Teatro Estudio Uniandes. LaurA is associate artist for Pan Pan Theatre Company 2024/2025 and the secretary of the Irish Society of Performance Designers (ISPD).

Suzie Cummins is a Dublin-based lighting designer for theatre, dance and events. She has worked as a designer in Ireland for almost a decade. Suzie was the 2023 recipient of Druid's Marie Mullen Bursary, an award for female theatre artists working in the fields of design, directing and dramaturgy. Suzie was the associate lighting designer on the *DruidO'Casey* trilogy in 2023. Lighting design credits include: *Super Bogger, Danty Dan, Tarry Flynn, Trad* (Livin' Dred); *Lost Lear, The Wrens* (Dan Colley and Riverbank); *The Making of Mollie, The Race* (The Ark); *Absent the Wrong* (Once Off Productions); *Every Brilliant Thing* (Abbey Theatre); *After Taste* (National Youth Theatre/Abbey Theatre); *The Secrets of Primrose Square* (Pat Moylan Productions); *Minseach* (Sibéal Davitt); *Before You Say Anything* (Malaprop); *Minefield, Charlie's a Clepto* (Clare Monnelly); *Harder, Faster More* (Red Bear). Associate lighting design credits include: *The Giggler Treatment* (The Ark); *Party Scene* (Thisispopbaby); *Solar Bones* (Rough Magic).

Denis Clohessy has worked with the Abbey Theatre, the Gate Theatre, Once Off Productions, Junk Ensemble, Coiscéim, Rough Magic, Fishamble, Corn Exchange, Northlight Theatre, Chicago and Beijing Children's Art Theatre. He won the Irish Times theatre award for Best Soundscape in 2011 and 2019. He was also a nominee in 2015 for Junk Ensemble and Brokentalker's *It Folds*. Denis was an associate artist with the Abbey in 2008 and was a participant on Rough Magic's ADVANCE programme in 2012.

Composition for film and television includes: the feature films *One Night in Millstreet* (Fastnet Films); *The Hum and The Confessors* (Atom Films); *Older Than Ireland* (Snackbox Films); *His and Hers* (Venom Film); *The Irish Pub* (Atom Films); *The Land of the Enlightened* (Savage Film); *In View* (Underground Cinema); *The Reluctant Revolutionary* (Underground Films); the television series *The Limits of Liberty* (South Wind Blows) performed by the RTE Concert Orchestra and the Will Sliney (Marvel Comics) animation series *Storytellers* (Fastnet Films).

Neil O'Driscoll designs video for stage whilst maintaining a practice as an illustrator and filmmaker. His recent theatre work includes: *Fun Home* (The Gate, Dublin); *Burnt Out* (The Lyric, Belfast); *Palimpsest* (The Complex, Dublin) and *The Summer I Robbed A Bank* (The Everyman, Cork). Having completed a degree in Film and TV at Edinburgh College of Art in 2008, following certificates in animation and crafts, Neil worked as a freelance illustrator whilst writing and directing independent films. Following a request to design set and video for *Happy End* (dir. Jimmy Fay) in 2012, he moved into video design, often integrating drawing and other handmade elements into his theatre work.

Cally Shine is a theatre producer from Seattle, WA, based in Dublin. She holds a BA in Theatre and a Minor in Irish Studies from the University of Montana and a Graduate Diploma in Cultural Policy and Arts Management from University College Dublin.

For Once Off Productions: *Rescue Annie* by Eoghan Carrick and Lauren Shannon Jones (Dublin Fringe Festival 2021); The Performance Corporation's *Emperor 101* (Dublin Theatre Festival 2021); *Looking For América* by Federico Julián González and Janet Moran (Edinburgh Festival

Fringe 2021, and Irish Tour 2022); *Absent the Wrong* by Carys D. Coburn (winner Best Production, Dublin Fringe Festival 2022); *Quake* by Janet Moran (Dublin Theatre Festival 2023, Zebbie Award Nominee 2024); *The United States v. Ulysses* by Colin Murphy (World Premier 2023, Zebbie Award Nominee 2024); *You Belong To Me* by Rory Nolan (World Premier 2023); *Elsewhere* by Michael Gallen (Irish Tour 2024); *Afterwards* by Janet Moran (Dublin Fringe Festival 2024); *Guest Host Stranger Ghost* by Kate Heffernan (Dublin Theatre Festival 2024).

For Fishamble: The New Play Company: *Duck Duck Goose* by Caitríona Daly (world premier and Irish tour 2021); *The Treaty* by Colin Murphy (world premier and international tour 2021); *Outrage* by Deirdre Kinahan (World Premier 2021 and Irish tour 2024); *Heaven* by Eugene O'Brien (world premier, Irish tour 2022, Off Broadway Transfer and Edinburgh Festival Fringe 2023); *KING* by Pat Kinevane (world premier, Irish tour, Edinburgh Festival Fringe 2023, and North American tour 2024); *The Humours of Bandon* by Margaret McAuliffe (North American tour 2023).

For Dead Centre: *Chekhov's First Play* by Dead Centre (international tour 2022).

Zoë Reynolds is a theatre stage manager and production coordinator for screen. Her most recent credits include *Unspeakable Conversations* by Christian O'Reilly in collaboration with Liz Carr, Mat Fraser and Olwen Fouéré (GIAF/Once Off Productions); *A Suburban Legend* by Caitríona Ní Mhurchú (Little Wolf Productions); *Elsewhere* by Michael Gallen (Remount tour with Straymaker/Once Off Productions); *Brennan's Bread TVC* (Butter Productions); *Sive* by John B. Keane (Gaiety Theatre); *The United States vs Ulysses* by Colin Murphy (Once Off Productions); *Quake* by Janet Moran (Once Off Productions); *The Local* by Medb Lambert, Clare Monnelly and Emma O'Grady (Asylum Productions/Once Off Productions); *Masterclass* by Terence McNally (Smock Alley Theatre/Once Off Productions); *Tonic* by Fionn Foley (Rough Magic) and *Daughter of God* (Asylum Productions/Once Off Productions).

Morgan Steele is a theatre administrator and producer originally from Los Angeles, California. She has worked internationally on both nonprofit and commercial productions within the US, Ireland, UK and Canada. Notable work in North America includes: the pre-Broadway tour of *Ain't Too Proud* (2018) and serving as the company manager on multiple shows at Berkeley Repertory Theatre. Ireland and UK projects include *Once* (Landmark Productions, 2017) and *Medicine* by Enda Walsh (Galway International Arts Festival and Edinburgh International Festival, 2021); *Book of Names* by Louise Lowe (Dublin Theatre Festival, 2021) and *Daughter of God* by Roderick Ford (Once Off and Asylum Productions, 2023). Morgan has also worked in the television industry as an associate producer for Disney Channel Media Relations. She holds a BA in Theatre and Performance Studies from UC Berkeley and an MSc in Business Management from Trinity College Dublin.

Sarah Purcell has worked in stage management for the last ten years. Some of her stage management/ASM credits include: *Circle Mirror Transformation* (Gate Theatre 2024); *Cinderella* (Gaiety Theatre 2023); *The Loved Ones* (Gate Theatre 2023); *Fun Home* (Gate Theatre 2023); *The Wrens* (Dan Colley 2023); *Gold in the Water* (Project Arts Centre 2023); *The Jungle Book* (Gaiety Theatre 2022); *A Very Old Man With Enormous Wings* (Irish tour); *Lost Lear* (Dan Colley 2022); *Circle of Friends* (Gaiety Theatre 2022).

Founded in 2006 by Maura O'Keeffe, **Once Off Productions** provides a structured, supportive and creative producing platform for independent performance artists making ambitious, innovative and collaborative work as well as professional development opportunities for freelance producers. Working nationally and internationally at all scales, the company is committed to bringing live performance to audiences in traditional and non-traditional locations.

Once Off Productions facilitates artists to make work outside of traditional company structures while simultaneously offering all of the advantages of producing and administrative support, enabling some of the most brilliant and exciting artists based in Ireland to create, develop and present new work for a wide range of audiences.

Led by a small team of experienced cultural sector professionals, Once Off Productions is a key part of the performing arts landscape in Ireland, nurturing artists and producers and fostering the development of innovative, collaborative, courageous and ambitious projects while marrying this work with the needs of presenters to serve audiences across the island of Ireland and internationally.

Acknowledgements

Thanks to the following for their help with this production: all at the Abbey Theatre; David Parnell, Liz Meany, Bea Kelleher and all at the Arts Council; Emma Rose Creaner; David Francis Moore, Bee Sparks and all at Dublin Fringe Festival; Emmett Farrell; Jim Culleton, Gavin Kostick, Laura MacNaughton and all at Fishamble; Niamh O'Donnell and all at Irish Theatre Institute; Amy Kidd; the students of the Lir Academy; Julie Kelleher and all at Mermaid Arts Centre; Conall Morrison; Michael Nevill; Maura O'Keeffe, Cally Shine and all at Once Off Productions; Nathan Snow; Nima Taleghani; Karen, Barry, Kevin, Esmé, Minna, Joe, Sam Fede (cdmym) and the wisest person I know and my greatest inspiration Ben Julián Moran; all those who helped since this publication went to print.

Afterwards

For Mick and Gemma,
Who do everything they can,
to give us everything we need.

Characters

Young Woman, *early 20s*
English Woman, *early 30s*
Cork Woman, *early 40s*
Young Man, *early 20s*
Orderly, *20s/30s*
Voice of doctor

Act One

Afternoon.

In the darkness, we hear a high pitched man's voice giving orders. Unintelligible, screechy, distorted. It rises.

Lights up on three beds, with three women lying in them. It's a clinical, bare, liminal space. At the back, a large white wall which can act as a screen or perhaps three white walls. During the play, projections can transform the space, perhaps to a bedroom, an outdoor space and can be used in transitions. It should feel as if we are looking in at the women through a window. As the pitch and volume of the man's voice rises, the young woman in the middle bed sits up, terrified. The voice stops.

Young Woman   A mad man. Is that a mad man? Run. Run.

The two women either side sit up, look at the **Young Woman** *and then lie back down. The* **Young Woman** *seems to swoon, then lies back down, lights flicker. She sits up abruptly again.*

He's dangerous. Run!

One of the other women giggles. Lights flicker like eyelids and down.

Lights up.

The two older women are sitting comfortably in their beds, reading magazines / on phones. The **Young Woman** *in the middle, sits up again, looks at the two women. They stop what they're doing and look at her. A moment? She lies back down again. They continue. Lights flicker again and down.*

Lights up.

The two women are chatting, one is now standing by the bed and the other is sitting with her feet out. The **Young Woman** *in the middle is still lying very flat on her back but is listening now to the women and occasionally moving her head.*

Cork Woman   Yeah, I could see everyone looking at me when my mum dropped me off.

English Woman   Well, to be fair, we were all thinking, 'her mum knows where she is?'.

Cork Woman *laughs.*

Cork Woman   Oh she does.

Beat. They look at the **Young Woman** *who is still lying flat and motionless.*

Cork Woman (*to* **Young Woman**)   You know, you can move around.

No response.

Love, you know you don't have to lie so still.

The **Young Woman** *moves her head slightly.*

Young Woman   Me?

Cork Woman   Yeah, you can move.

Young Woman   Is it safe?

The two older women look at each other and laugh a little.

English Woman   Yes. What are you afraid of?

Young Woman   I don't know. (*Beat.*) Maybe I'll damage myself?

Cork Woman   Sit up, love.

The **Young Woman** *struggles gingerly to half sitting.*

Cork Woman   You OK?

Young Woman   Yeah, I feel funny.

Beat.

Cork Woman   Lie back down, sure.

She does.

Beat.

English Woman   I'm fucking starving, are you?

Cork Woman   Yeah. Oh, I have some jellies. Do you want one?

English Woman   Oh, yes please.

She walks over to the **Cork Woman***'s bed and chooses a jelly.*

Cork Woman   Love, do you want a jelly?

Young Woman   Yes please.

Cork Woman *walks to* **Young Woman***'s bed and puts a jelly in her mouth.* **Young Woman** *lies flat, chewing.* **Cork Woman** *looks to* **English Woman**. *They shrug. She stays by the bed, feeding jellies to the* **Young Woman**.

English Woman   So where are you staying at?

Cork Woman   In Sudbury. Awful kip. Well, my mum's place is nice.

English Woman   Oh, your mum lives *here?*

Cork Woman   Yeah, she moved just a few years ago.

English Woman   Oh yeah? How come?

Cork Woman   She met an English man on holidays and decided to give it a go.

English Woman   Whaaaaaat? How old was she?

Cork Woman   In her late sixties when she met him. Not long after my dad died.

English Woman   Go on.

Cork Woman   Yeah. She's no wallflower, my mum. She'll keep living her life right till the end.

English Woman   What's her name?

Cork Woman (*beat, like she's making up the name*)   Maureen.

English Woman   Go on, Maureen. Chapeau.

Cork Woman *smiles thinly.*

Beat.

Cork Woman   Where do you live?

English Woman   Balham. It's alright. Close to work.

Cork Woman   What do you do?

English Woman   Training to be a solicitor.

Cork Woman   Very good.

English Woman   Yeah, it will be. I hope.

There is the low hum of prayers outside. **English Woman** *goes to window at front and looks out.*

English Woman   There's loads out there now.

Cork Woman   Fuckers.

Young Woman (*re. the jellies*)   Thanks, that's enough.

Cork Woman, *straining to look out window, doesn't hear her and shoves another in her mouth. She's a bit startled. Mouth full of jellies.*

Cork Woman   Wouldn't you think they have someone else to be bothering.

English Woman   Like who?

Cork Woman   I don't know. Foreigners?

English Woman   Oh, I'd say they do them too.

Cork Woman   I bet they do.

She stuffs another jelly in **Young Woman**'s *mouth*

Young Woman (*choking*)   Sorry. That's grand. Thanks.

Cork Woman   OK, love.

She goes back to her bed. **Young Woman** *woozily sits up, looks around.*

Young Woman (*to* **Cork Woman**)   Was your mum with you?

English Woman (*laughs*)   I know.

Cork Woman   Yeah.

Young Woman   Huh. I wish mine was.

Cork Woman   Could you not tell her?

The **Young Woman** *shakes her head.*

Young Woman   No.

English Woman   I'm bloody glad my mum's not here. She'd be causing all kinds of ructions.

Young Woman   Would she?

English Woman   Oh yeah, she'd string me up. Just for being irresponsible and that. Wouldn't yours?

Young Woman   No. I don't know. She'd just be really upset.

English Woman (*pause*)   Yeah.

Cork Woman   Did you come on your own?

Young Woman   No, my friend brought me.

English Woman   Is he the . . .?

Young Woman   No, he's my friend.

Cork Woman   That's a good friend.

Young Woman   Yeah, he lent me the money and paid for the boat.

Cork Woman   Ah, the traditional route. Ya know the plane is cheaper now though, don't you?

Young Woman   Oh, is it? I, I just . . . oh.

Cork Woman *gently shakes her head.*

Cork Woman   What about you?

English Woman   Oh, I just got the Tube over.

Cork Woman   I flew this morning.

Beat.

English Woman (*realising*)   Sorry. But. Why are you *here*?

Cork Woman   What? I would have thought that was self-evident. No?

English Woman   No, I mean, *here*. Don't you guys have abortion now in Ireland?

Cork Woman   Oh yeah. We do. Well. kind of.

English Woman   What do you mean kind of?

Cork Woman   Well, up to a point.

English Woman   Oh right. Yeah. I remember seeing it on Gogglebox. I was watching it. All these women cheering and crying and dancing in a big 'castle' place? I was like that's weird. They must really like abortions there.

Cork Woman   Well. I don't know about like.

English Woman   Well, want abortions.

Cork Woman   Well. Obviously.

English Woman   So why come here?

Cork Woman   Eh. Well, Ireland's a small country, ya know. And I didn't want my doctor to know.

English Woman   You didn't want your doctor to know? But wouldn't it be confidential?

Cork Woman *looks at her, sideways.*

English Woman   Oooohhhhh. Right.

English Woman *looks over at* **Young Woman**.

English Woman   And what about you?

Young Woman   Eh, I. I. I was a bit slow to realise what was happening.

English Woman   So?

Cork Woman   You can only get an abortion up to twelve weeks in Ireland. After that it's exceptional circumstances

English Woman   What's exceptional circumstances?

Young Woman   Eh. I don't know.

Cork Woman   Risk to life? Maybe . . .

English Woman   Well, that's arguable, isn't it? I mean, it's actually a criminal offence to get an abortion here in the UK.

Young Woman *looks startled*.

Young Woman   What?

Cork Woman   What do you mean criminal?

English Woman   I mean it's only *de facto* legal. It's only because the grounds of risk of injury to mental health is interpreted liberally that it happens. It's not a right. Like you *could* be prosecuted. Technically.

Young Woman *looks terrified*.

Cork Woman   Wow. I didn't know.

English Woman   Yeah, so just saying. You know. You can't take it for granted.

Cork Woman   That's mad.

English Woman   Yeah. I mean we're not in America so /

Cork Woman   / Thank God.

English Woman   . . . it's probably OK to take it for granted . . .?

Cork Woman   I think America's exactly why you can't take it for granted . . .

English Woman   Ta . . . rue . . .

Beat.

(*To* **Young Woman**.) So what? You were too late?

Young Woman   Yeah, I suppose

English Woman   Why? Did you not realise? That you were pregnant.

Young Woman   Em, I was kind of in denial maybe. When I went to the doctor, I just went cos I was sleeping all the time. She made me take a pregnancy test. It came back positive. She asked me when was my last period and I told her. But, I wasn't really sure of the dates so I kind of guessed. And she said that's not good enough. And then, because they make you take a three day "cooling off period" as well, she said there was no point. She reckoned I was past the twelve week cut off point anyway or eighty-four days, I think, is the limit. I *thought* I was seventy something days but she said no. She said I'd have to start getting my head around being a mother and that behaving responsibly would be a good start.

Cork Woman   Did she really?

Young Woman   Yeah. So, I was kind of a bit out of it then, I didn't really know what to do, but then I met up with my friend from college, the one who brought me over and I guess he knew there was something wrong with me. So, I told him and he said he'd help me get over here. He has a job. And I don't. Yet. But he had to save for a bit. So . . . I'm gonna pay him back.

Cork Woman   Ah. It's not nothing either, right? Having to stay overnight when you're further along and everything.

Young Woman   Yeah.

English Woman   Good for him.

English Woman *thinks for a moment*.

What was it *called*?

Young Woman   Wha . . . the baby?

Cork Woman   What?

English Woman   Fuck no. The movement. To get abortion.

Cork Woman   Oh. Repeal.

English Woman   That's right. Repeal.

Beat.

Young Woman   I was there. In the castle.

English Woman   That was on TV?

Young Woman   Yeah. It was mad. We got the bus into town. But I had Ceoltairí, music group all day. So when me and my friends got into town, it was mostly all over. We went into the courtyard of Dublin Castle and there was just little groups of people standing around. Some crying. And in the middle there was a circle of women all linked and they were singing. We just watched them for a while and then we went home.

English Woman   Did you vote?

Young Woman   No, like I was only fourteen then. And so, we couldn't go anywhere. We just went home. We were kind of dazed on the bus.

English Woman (*to* **Cork Woman**)   Did you vote?

Cork Woman   Yeah, of course I did.

Young Woman   What did you vote?

Cork Woman   Well, now what do you think I voted?

Young Woman (*uncertainly*)   Yes?

Cork Woman   Yes. It was a good day. I'd had a good feeling about it beforehand but still it was a relief.

English Woman   Why'd you have a good feeling?

Cork Woman   Just from going on one or two marches. Seeing the young women. They're different now.

Young Woman   Different? How?

Cork Woman   Just . . . I don't know. You're better in a lot of
ways. I remember when I was a young teenager, even the
idea of abortion embarrassed me. Anything like that.
Anything that singled me out as a woman. (*She makes a face.*)
I think I wouldn't have ever wanted to talk about it or
acknowledge it. But on the marches, all the young ones out
with their banners and their chants, urging, expecting,
demanding. I found it very moving you know. There's a lot
less shame. It's good.

Pause.

Cork Woman *laughs.*

Like we were so clueless really. I remember going up to
Dublin shopping with my mother when I was a kid and we
went into the Virgin Megastore to look at the condoms, cos
they had just been legalised. Like we went in to just *look* at
them. Amazed like.

She laughs again lightly. To **Young Woman**.

Cork Woman   And do you remember Home to Vote?

Young Woman   No.

Cork Woman   All the people flying home. It was on the
news. All these people coming from all over the world.
Arriving in Dublin airport with their Repeal jumpers.
Smiling. Coming from Brussels, here, Saudi Arabia even. It
was incredible.

Young Woman   Oh yeah, didn't they do that for the
marriage referendum as well.

Cork Woman   Yeah.

Young Woman   Yeah, we couldn't vote for that either. We
missed all the good referendums.

Cork Woman   Ah, there might be more. There's surely
other things to improve in Ireland, wouldn't ya say?

Young Woman *nods emphatically.*

Cork Woman   They were good though. All the solidarity. Ya know? Those moments when people are given a chance to show . . . care. And they do. We don't get those chances that often. But when we do . . . Sometimes we surprise ourselves.

Beat.

English Woman   Still have to keep it a secret though, eh?

Cork Woman   Yeah.

Young Woman   Yeah.

Silence.

Cork Woman   I said I wanted to visit my mum and do a bit of shopping.

Young Woman   I said we were coming for a gig.

English Woman   I didn't say anything. I didn't expect to stay overnight either so hopefully it'll all be OK.

Cork Woman   Why *did* you have to stay?

English Woman   I don't know really. They wanted to keep me in for observation or something.

They keep looking at her.

English Woman   Annoying.

Cork Woman   Right. (*Beat.*) I suppose I'll have to do some shopping. Get stuff for the kids anyway.

Young Woman   You have kids?

Cork Woman   Yeah, my husband is minding them.

Both Women   Your husband?

Cork Woman   Yeah.

Young Woman   Your husband is minding the kids?

Cork Woman   Yes.

Beat.

English Woman   It's a pity he couldn't come with you.

Cork Woman   Well, I didn't tell him.

Beat.

Young Woman   You didn't tell him?

Cork Woman   No. I didn't tell him.

Young Woman   Oh.

Cork Woman *stares at her.*

Cork Woman   Is that a problem?

Young Woman   No. (*It clearly is.*)

Pause.

Cork Woman   I couldn't. There was no point. In hurting him. Unfortunately, it just wasn't going to work out.

English Woman   The pregnancy?

Cork Woman   Yeah.

English Woman   Oh, I'm sorry. That's hard.

Cork Woman   Mmmh.

Young Woman   How many kids do you have?

Cork Woman   Three boys. My husband would love a girl. He'd *really* love a girl, but . . .

Pause.

Cork Woman   What about you?

English Woman   Oh, I had a one night stand. Actually to be honest, I really liked him. We work together a bit. Like he's in the same firm but in a different sort of area. We went for work drinks and more drinks and blah blah blah. (*Thinks.*) It was really nice. I've liked him for ages. We had such a laugh at the drinks thing. Like proper clicked. Then when we were leaving, he just grabbed my hand and said, 'You're not going home yet', and on we went to a club, danced all night. A lot of laughing. You know the way. Then we staggered home and he just came in. It really *seemed* like he was crazy about me.

Cork Woman   That doesn't *sound* like a one night stand.

English Woman   No, well, the next day, he just . . . left, you know. He wasn't interested. Like, he made that pretty clear. Any time I bumped into him then, in the office, he just wouldn't meet my eye, like didn't even want to say hello. It was pretty humiliating really cos I thought we'd had a nice time. Like I wouldn't have slept with him, only I thought he liked me, you know. I must be a really bad shag, eh?

Beat.

Well, then I found out that I was, you know. And it didn't really seem like it was something I could tell him about. It's not like he was going to be a great support.

Young Woman   He might have helped you.

English Woman (*thinks*)   He wouldn't have. He definitely wouldn't have. I mean, I can't even rely on him to say hello to me in the office. So, like, you know? So, I came here.

Young Woman   He's a dick.

English Woman   Yeah, he is.

Cork Woman   What about you?

Young Woman   Em. Kinda similar. I went to a party. Someone had a bottle of whiskey. I'd never drank it before.

English Woman   Oh!

Silence. They look at **Young Woman** *expectantly.*

English Woman   So?

Young Woman   Oh, yeah, so, I don't really remember anything about it.

Cork Woman   What do you mean?

Young Woman   Well, I remember leaving and my friend was telling a friend of a friend that he should get me home safe. I remember my friend was laughing at how drunk I was. I couldn't really stand, they were holding me up.

Cork Woman   Why didn't he bring you home?

Young Woman   I don't know. I don't really know why they told *him* to bring me home. I don't even know him. I guess everyone was pretty drunk. I think maybe, we were going the same way? I remember being in a taxi and then the next thing . . .

English Woman   What?

Young Woman *takes a deep breath.*

Young Woman   Em. I remember I was lying on a mattress on a floor and the guy was on top of me. (*She looks down and gives a little embarrassed laugh, then rapidly.*) Anyway, the next morning, I just got up and left. It was on North Circular road. It was freezing and I walked back into town and got the bus back to my mum's. Straight away, I felt different somehow. I didn't know but I think maybe deep down I knew. And I felt sick right from that day. But I just kind of zoned out or something. Funny thing is though when I did the counselling session here, they did a pregnancy test and I was still shocked when she said I was pregnant. I was hoping she would tell me I'd made a mistake. But I hadn't. It was weird. She did the pregnancy test, then she came back in the room and she just sat there looking at me. She didn't say anything. Then I said am I pregnant and she laughed and said yeah. I started crying and she just sat there looking at me. I wanted to punch her. And that was it.

The two other women stare at her.

English Woman   Babe, that's not similar.

Cork Woman   Love /

/ Noise of children laughing, shouting etc outside. They turn to window.

Cork Woman   Is that a *school* getting out?

She goes to window and looks out.

English Woman   Fucking hell, now that is weird.

English Woman *goes to window.*

Cork Woman   What is it?

English Woman   I don't know. Are they going on a tour or something?

Cork Woman   Ah, look at them all holding hands.

English Woman   In their little pairs.

They watch for a moment.

Young Woman   I think I'll have a nap.

She lies down. The other two women look at each other.

Cork Woman   I'm going for a fag.

English Woman   Where do you go?

Cork Woman   No idea, I'll find out.

She leaves.

English Woman *begins to read her magazine.* **Young Woman** *sits up.*

Young Woman   What did she mean, the pregnancy wasn't going to work out?

English Woman   Oh, I imagine there was some kind of problem that the child wouldn't survive. Fatal foetal, I think they call it.

Young Woman   Oh.

English Woman   Really sad.

Young Woman   Strange that she didn't tell her husband.

English Woman   How?

Young Woman   That she wouldn't want his support.

English Woman   I guess maybe, she really loves him and was trying to spare him the pain.

Young Woman   Yeah. (*Pause.*) I'm gonna have that nap.

Cork Woman *returns.*

Cork Woman   Fuckin hell. I can't find my way out of here and there's no one to ask. I'm gumming. (*Beat.*) I don't want to go out the front.

She stands at the door looking into the hall.

English Woman   Oh, just have one out the window.

Cork Woman   Nah, I'll wait.

She climbs back into bed. Her phone rings.

Cork Woman   Mum!

Good, good. Fine.

They whisper together for a bit.

Thanks.

Pause. Then, louder, nodding towards the other two.

The other two girls were slagging me because you were here earlier. They couldn't believe I'd told my mum.

She listens.

(*To women.*) She says she wouldn't be one for judging. (*To phone.*) I suppose *you* couldn't. (*Beat.*) Sorry. I know. Yeah I'll see you tomorrow. Love you too.

She hangs up.

Cork Woman   Oh. Maybe that was a bit close to the bone.

Young Woman   Why?

Cork Woman   Well, saying that she couldn't be judging us. She's been down this road herself.

Young Woman   Did she have an . . .

Cork Woman   Wise up. She got pregnant when she was sixteen. What like fifty-odd years ago. She had the child and then she was taken from her.

Young Woman *sits up.*

Young Woman   Why was the baby taken from her?

Cork Woman   Because she wasn't married. Have you never read a history book?

Young Woman (*annoyed*)   Well, it's not actually *in* the history books.

Cork Woman *concedes this.*

Cork Woman   Fair enough, that's true.

English Woman   Where was she taken?

Cork Woman   Your guess is as good as mine. She had her in a mother and baby home. She had her for five months there. And then one day baby was just gone. Adopted they said. And that's all they said. Cunts

English Woman   Who the *nuns*?

Cork Woman   Yes. Cunts.

English Woman *makes a shocked face and laughs.*

Silence.

Cork Woman   Funny to think I have a sister somewhere.

English Woman   Did you never look for her.

Cork Woman   Nah. Maybe I should. Anyway, poor mum really didn't have a choice.

Young Woman   Just like you.

Cork Woman   What do you mean?

Young Woman   You didn't have a choice either.

Cork Woman   What do you mean?

Young Woman   Well, your baby was going to die.

Cork Woman   What?

Young Woman   Did you not . . .?

She looks to **English Woman**.

Cork Woman   What?

English Woman *looks at the floor.*

Cork Woman   What?

Young Woman   I thought you said that it wasn't going to work out.

Cork Woman   It wasn't.

Young Woman   Because of foetal . . .

English Woman   Fuck sake. Sorry, maybe we misunderstood you.

Cork Woman   Fatal foetal?

Young Woman   Yes.

Cork Woman   No. No. It wasn't going to work out because I didn't want another child. I'm just getting my life back after having the three lads.

Young Woman   And you didn't . . .?

Cork Woman   What?

Young Woman (*timidly*)   Tell your husband?

Cork Woman   No. He would have stopped me. And if he finds out, he'll probably leave me.

Young Woman   No, he wouldn't.

Cork Woman *looks at her in amazement.*

Cork Woman   Shut. Up. It's not something I did lightly, I can tell you. I literally couldn't face it again. I got so depressed. I felt an actual physical revulsion.

Young Woman   Oh, so did I! I felt a physical revulsion. That's weird isn't it?

English Woman *looks at her sideways.*

English Woman   Not really.

Young Woman   I felt like I was invaded by an alien. Did you?

Cork Woman   Emm, kind of. Anyway, we felt the same right?

Young Woman   Yeah.

Cork Woman   So it wasn't gonna work out. I couldn't continue. I couldn't tell him. So I rang my mum and she organised it for me.

Young Woman   Aren't you worried he'll find out?

Cork Woman   Are *you* gonna tell him?

Young Woman   No. No.

Silence.

Cork Woman   Anyway, why don't you tell the police you were raped?

Young Woman   Fuck sake. No, I wasn't. Fuck sake.

A mobile phone rings.

Young Woman   It's my mum.

The phone rings and rings. She looks at it.

English Woman   Answer it.

Young Woman *looks at her.*

The phone continues to ring and ring.

Video design in transition that speaks to the day, the travel, somewhat abstract.

Act Two

Evening.

Back in the ward.

A young man enters with a parcel. He looks at **English Woman** *and* **Cork Woman** *and nods quite formally. They nod back equally stiffly. He walks to the* **Young Woman** *and sits by her bed. The two older women, watch discreetly.*

Young Man   Hello.

Young Woman   Hello.

She slowly sits up.

Young Man   How are you feeling?

Young Woman   OK.

Young Man   I got you this.

She opens the parcel. It is a glass paraffin lamp.

Young Woman   Thanks.

She is a bit nonplussed.

Young Woman   It's lovely.

Young Man   I bought it in a second hand shop near here. And I got you a Boost.

Young Woman   Thanks.

He gives the chocolate bar to her. She holds it in her hand.

Young Man   Are you feeling relieved?

Young Woman   I don't know.

Young Man   You did the right thing.

Young Woman   Hmm.

Young Man   Do you know there's a really nice park near here as well. We could go there tomorrow. Afterwards.

Young Woman   Maybe, yeah.

Young Man   Would you like to go to see a film tomorrow?

Young Woman   Maybe, yeah.

Young Man   We could meet up with Nora and some of the others.

Young Woman   Emm, maybe not.

Young Man   Cool.

They sit in silence for a bit.

Young Woman   What did you do today?

Young Man   I went to the Science Museum. It was fascinating actually. You know what scurvy is right?

Young Woman   Yes.

Young Man   So, it's caused by a lack of vitamin C. But did you know that without vitamin C, we cannot produce collagen. See, collagen is an essential component of bones, cartilage and other connective tissues. It binds our wounds whenever we're cut or bruised or whatever BUT that binding is continually being replaced throughout our lives. Which is the bit I didn't know. You're always 're-healing'. So like in advanced scurvy, old wounds, that were healed can reappear. So, even a person's oldest injuries are never really gone. Our bodies are walking, talking archives of injuries. Isn't that mad?

She stares at him.

Young Woman   Yeah. It is.

He looks awkward.

Young Man   I mean, obviously we're more than that too so . . .

She looks at her lamp.

Young Man   And there was an exhibition about hydro power where you could have a go at making water generate electricity. I was well into it, before I realised it was only for kids. I was getting proper dirty looks from the mums all around. And this little fella says to me 'Get lost big boy' I said 'I will, little boy, I will'. So I legged it. Completely soaked by the way. I had to go back to the hostel to change. Eejit.

She smiles.

The other two women are listening intently.

Noises off of dinners being served.

Young Man   I better go, eh, let you have your dinner.

Young Woman   Yeah.

Young Man   I'm heading out tonight. Some of the guys are going to a gig. We'll miss you.

Young Woman   Don't tell them I'm here.

Young Man   Oh no, no of course not. Well. I'll be back in the morning to get you.

Young Woman   Yep.

He gets up.

Young Man   Well, sleep well. See you tomorrow.

Young Woman   Thank you. Thank you so much.

Young Man   Oh for nothing. Good night, ladies.

Both Women   Goodnight.

He leaves.

Cork Woman   Well, that cheered you up a bit, did it?

Young Woman   Yeah.

Cork Woman   Where's he staying?

Young Woman   We're staying in a hostel. He's got friends here though.

Young Man *comes back in hurriedly and goes to* **Young Woman**'s *bedside again.*

Young Man   I'm really sorry.

Young Woman   What? For what?

He looks down at his shoes.

Young Man   I feel like it's my fault.

Young Woman   What? Why?

Young Man   I shouldn't have let that guy take you home. I didn't know . . . that he was such a creep.

Young Woman *looks towards the other women sharply.*

Young Woman   Don't be stupid. I mean. It's not your fault.

Young Man   But I /

Young Woman   / Jesus, you're ALL so keen to turn me into a victim . . . I'm not.

Young Man *confusedly looks at the other two women.*

Young Man   No, I'm not. I'm not. I'm just sorry. That's all. I'll see you tomorrow.

Young Woman   See you tomorrow. Here, will you take this actually? It's all melted.

She hands him the Boost all squashed from her hand.

She smiles at him weakly.

Young Woman   Have a good time tonight.

Young Man   I will. Bye.

He leaves.

Silence, nobody knows what to say.

Distant sound off of man's voice down a hall somewhere.

Doctor's Voice   I'm off now. Goodnight. See you tomorrow bright and early.

Young Woman *starts.*

Young Woman   Who is that?

English Woman   It's the doctor.

Young Woman   Oh.

English Woman   'Run, run, there's a mad man.'

English Woman *and* **Cork Woman** *laugh.* **Young Woman** *stares at them and then begins to smile. Then laughs.*

The three of them begin to laugh hysterically. The **Young Woman** *is rolling around laughing.*

Young Woman   I'm such a dick.

Cork Woman   Ah no, he does sound strange.

Young Woman *laughs and laughs, the other women's laughing falls away and they realise the* **Young Woman** *is crying hard, loud sobs. She cries till she stops, hacking, slowing, stops.*

Young Woman   I don't want to be here.

Cork Woman   Nobody does.

Orderly *comes in with dinner. He's young, cool, Indian immigrant. The women get out of their beds and sit in the seats beside the beds.*

Orderly   Well ladies, teas's up. If you want to sit at your tables. Scrambled eggs and toast. Only the best, eh?

He goes out.

English Woman   Bloody hell.

The three women get out of bed and sit beside the tables.

Orderly *walks in with plates.*

Cork Woman   Is there somewhere I can go for a cigarette?

Orderly   Oh, I wouldn't go outside just now, mate. There's quite a crowd. Avoid it.

The three women fall silent. He throws his eyes up theatrically.

Nothing better to do, eh?

He finishes up.

Well, eat up all that dinner, ladies. You need your strength. It's been a long day, right?

Cork Woman   Yeah. Was up at five for the flight.

Orderly   You Irish?

Cork Woman   Yeah. So's she.

Orderly   Oh, you know each other?

Cork Woman (*sighs*)   No.

Orderly   We *still* get so many Irish. Oh my days. I thought things was all changed over there.

Pause.

Cork Woman   Kind of.

Orderly   Huh. My partner's Irish. We're even thinking of moving there. Cos you know, it feels like here, right now, we're going in the wrong direction.

Cork Woman   Yeah, that's all a bit strange, isn't it?

Orderly   Oh, you telling me? What is wrong with these English at all?

Young Woman   Are you not English?

Orderly   I am not, young lady. I am a British citizen but I am Indian. Indo/English. (*Beat.*) It's very different.

Cork Woman   Is it?

Orderly   Yes.

Young Woman   Sorry.

Orderly   You are forgiven.

Young Woman   I hope so.

Orderly *goes to window. We can hear the protesting/praying, it's louder than before.*

Orderly   Do you want me to draw these curtains?

Cork Woman   Nah, the street light is nice.

He looks out and gives a little wave.

Orderly   Hi, Mary.

Cork Woman   Mary?

Orderly   Oh yeah, I mean I know most of them now. It's a bit late for Mary now to be out though. She's old.

He mimes shivering out the window.

It's cold out there, Mary. Go home.

He mimes again.

Cold. Go home, mate. You gotta keep strong to come back shouting for another day.

He chuckles and shakes his head.

She's a determined one, Mary.

He turns around to see the three women staring at him.

Ah, they're just doing their thing, ladies.

English Woman   Doing their thing?

Orderly   They've got their beliefs, you know. (*He shrugs.*) It's a free country, innit? And they aren't the worst of them.

Cork Woman   They aren't ?

Orderly   Well, I mean as *protestors* go. There's a few different brigades going about these days. Protesting various things. It's a national pastime I think. And I feel a bit sorry for Mary, you know. She's a lonely one, I reckon. Maybe she would have liked a family of her own. She just don't understand it. I guess it's black and white for her. But, William out there now, he does get a bit hasty. I'm not keen. And then, Julia she's just mad religious so she's absolutely *certain* she's doing the right thing. Must be nice, that certainty.

He looks back out.

But yeah, you're right, they're arseholes really for doing that. I mean you're just doing *your* thing, ladies.

Young Woman   It's not really 'our thing'.

Orderly   Yeah, yeah of course. Sorry, mate.

Cork Woman (*gently*)   Ya know, ya might want to rethink moving to Ireland. A few different brigades there too.

Orderly   What do you mean?

Cork Woman *looks uncomfortable. She's not sure how to phrase it.*

Cork Woman   Just a lot of protests. Different ones.

Orderly *smiles.*

Orderly   Ha, don't worry about me. I'm well used to people holding opinions about me.

Cork Woman *nods.*

Cork Woman   I've no doubt.

English Woman (*sarcastically*)   This is delicious.

Cork Woman   Mmm, delicious like shite.

Orderly   You are welcome. I shall pass your compliments to the man who mixed the powdered eggs and milk. I better get on with dishing out delights.

He salutes them and leaves.

The three women pick at their food.

English Woman   Do you think they're punishing us.

Cork Woman   Yes, yes I do.

They all push their plates away and sit depressed.

English Woman   Tell you what. What's the best meal you ever had?

Young Woman   Em . . .

English Woman   OK, I'll go first. Em, my best meal was up in the Cotswolds. I'd gone to visit my grandparents. I hadn't seen them in ages, truth be told. But I just took a notion one day and drove up. Of course they were thrilled to see me but immediately thought something was wrong. It took ages to convince them I wasn't in the midst of a crisis. Anyway, I went for a walk with my grandad. And he forages. I didn't know that, but we went looking for mushrooms and wild garlic and we got all this stuff and went back and I helped my gran roast a lamb with all these herbs we'd found and a mushroom sauce for the potatoes and it was sensational and then afterwards we sat out in their garden and ate scones with clotted cream and jam. Outrageous. Outrageously good. Now you.

Young Woman   Em, my best thing is sitting on a roof in Pushkar in India last summer and eating yoghurt and pomegranate and realising that I was maybe the first of my people, of my family to be there.

English Woman   Ah, good one. Now you. Your best meal?

Cork Woman   My best meal? Hmm, my best meal. Funnily enough, it was probably the toast I had after the birth of my first son. I was ravenous. I had a caesarean and it wasn't expected so I just hadn't eaten that day and then it all was a bit of a rush.

Young Woman   How come you had a caesarean?

Cork Woman   He was breach so they'd been keeping an eye on me. So I had to come in for an extra scan three days before I was due to be sectioned but, then they realised that there was very little fluid around him. So suddenly, right at the last minute, there was a chance that I was going to lose him. It was terrifying, you know. I'd been carrying him for nine months, preparing, watching him move around my stomach and now as we were so close, he was in danger. So they decided to take me down for an emergency section. Now because we had thought it was a routine enough check up, my husband had gone to work. So I called him and said 'Can you come back, they're going to do a section in an hour'. So he was in a panic and of course it was rush hour traffic, all that stuff. My mum was with me though. She was fantastic. They prepped us for the surgery, you know, the caps and gowns and all that.

The funny thing is I wasn't scared at all once they were taking me in and because I knew I was going to meet him soon. I wasn't scared about being cut open. Not at all. I honestly felt like they could cut my legs off, I wouldn't mind, so long as he was OK. Course my mum was going through a different thing entirely because I was *her* baby and I was going to be cut open.

I don't know why but I took a photo of the two of us there, in our caps and gowns and it really is the most extraordinary photo. My face is just bursting with hope and happiness and expectation and right beside me, cheek to cheek, my mum is smiling but her eyes are bursting with tears and fear. Anyway, they brought me in and gave me the anaesthetic and then they called my mum who was going to be there with me, but the door opened and my husband rushed in. In his cap and gown. I don't know how he managed to get there so fast. It seemed like I'd only left my mum seconds before. He beamed in and then they cut me and because there was so little fluid around the baby, they couldn't get purchase on him or something so it was quite violent. It wasn't going well, they had to give more anaesthetic and I was lowing like a calf and I could feel their hands inside me. I could feel them starting to panic and then I started to panic but then I looked at my husband and he was so calm.

Like so calm. Just smiling at me as if we were just lolling around. And I thought, 'Oh it must be OK', if he is calm and I just gave myself over to it. The table was shaking, their hands were rooting around in me, I was being lifted and thrown, the table was shaking and we were just looking into each other's faces and smiling. And then all of a sudden, there he was, my son, being lifted in the air. And the first feeling I recognised when I glimpsed him was . . . shyness. I felt shy. Because somehow I thought I'd know him. I thought he'd be *mine*. But he wasn't. He was himself. Completely himself. And the only thing I could think was that I hoped he'd like me.

Silence. They take all this in. Then.

Young Woman (*timidly*)   Why didn't you tell your husband you were coming here?

Cork Woman (*hard*)   None of your fucking business.

Silence.

English Woman   Em, what about a song?

Cork Woman   It's not a fucking party.

English Woman   Life's what you make it, love.

Cork Woman (*to* **Young Woman**)   And you could do with being a little less judgmental. You know you're here too and it's not for a fucking holiday.

Young Woman   Sorry, it's just . . .

Cork Woman   What? It's just what?

Young Woman   Well, I wouldn't be here if I didn't have to be.

Silence. Slow build of rage in **Cork Woman**. **English Woman** *sees it.*

Cork Woman   You think I don't have to be?

Young Woman   Just, you're not on your own. I'm sorry.

Cork Woman   No, I'm not and I love my kids and I love my husband, but you don't know the toll it can take, having kids. I hope you get to find out someday. I hope you get to know, the physical toll, the fucking exhaustion. The losing of yourself. The loneliness. And then starting to feel that you are finally coming back to yourself. And then the absolute terror, the terror of facing into it all again. I don't have to explain myself to you, but I can tell you I could have lost everything if I'd had this child. My mental health, my marriage. *Nobody* should have to go through with an unwanted pregnancy and especially not because *you* think my situation is not bad enough to warrant having an abortion. It's none of your fucking business.

Young Woman   I'm really sorry. I just, I just, I just can't imagine anything worse than this right now.

Cork Woman   Well, believe me, there is. Try weeks of terror and indecision and stalling and stalling until it was too late for me to even do it at home even if I'd wanted to and having to hide it all from the people I love the most.

Silence.

English Woman   Anyone got a song?

Silence.

English Woman *starts to sing the first lines of 'Life's What You Make It' by Talk Talk, badly.*

Cork Woman   I'm going to sleep.

She lies down.

English Woman   Fancy a game of cards?

Young Woman   OK.

She walks over to **English Woman***'s bed, as she passes* **Cork Woman***.*

Young Woman   I'm sorry.

They sit and begin to play.

English Woman   Snap?

Young Woman (*nods*)   Do you feel different?

English Woman   Yes, I do. More like myself already.

Young Woman   Me too.

Pause.

Young Woman   Are you sorry you slept with that guy?

English Woman *gives her a look.*

English Woman (*laughs*)   Well, I won't be doing it again. (*Pause.*) I really liked him.

Young Woman   If it had worked out with him, would you have kept it?

English Woman   I don't think so. I'm just getting started with work. It would have been a disaster. I've worked really hard to get to where I am and it would have been all for nothing. You know.

Young Woman   Yeah.

English Woman   I mean, I would have been right back to the start. Do you know what I mean?

Young Woman   Yeah.

English Woman   Like, I've got to be able to do long days and work nights until I get established.

Young Woman   Yeah.

English Woman   Snap.

Young Woman   But you could have done it.

English Woman   What?

Young Woman   Like, you didn't have to do this.

English Woman   What do you mean?

Young Woman   I just mean, you have a job and your own place and the guy, like he probably would have given you money if you needed it. You might have lost time with work but you could have made it up. (*Beat.*) Couldn't you?

Silence.

English Woman   What the fuck is wrong with you?

Young Woman   What, nothing. I just . . . I just.

English Woman   Do you think you're the only one who has a right to be here, just because you were raped?

Young Woman   I wasn't raped.

English Woman   Oh Jesus, you really are a tonic. Did you like the guy?

Young Woman   Oh God no, He's gross.

English Woman   Did you want to be with him?

Young Woman   NO.

English Woman   Did you say yes to having sex with him?

Young Woman   No.

English Woman   But he had sex with you anyway.

Young Woman   I was too drunk to say yes. I mean . . . I was too drunk to say no . . .

English Woman   He fucking raped you. He saw that you were vulnerable. He took his chance because he probably knew you wouldn't touch him with a barge pole. And he fucking raped you. And I'm really sorry for you. But you need to fucking grow up.

Young Woman *is utterly deflated.*

Cork Woman   I'm going for a cigarette.

English Woman   Outside?

Cork Woman   Yeah, I don't care.

English Woman   I'll go with you.

They leave.

Young Woman *sits there for a bit. Her phone rings. She holds it for a while trying to decide whether to take it. Then suddenly answers. Big faux brightness performance.*

Young Woman   Hey, Mum. Yeah, I missed you earlier. We were out and about. Yeah, it's great. Yeah. We're good. Yeah, the hostel is nice. (*She looks up guiltily.*) Yeah, the other people staying here are nice. No, I won't. I won't, mum. I won't. Em, we went to the Science Museum. It was good. An exhibition about skin. I mean, about healing. About how you never really heal. And if you stop taking vitamin C, your wounds reopen. Yeah, they are. I said yes, our bodies ARE amazing. No, I'm fine. Honestly, I'm fine. I'm not sad. Em, he's just gone to the shop. No, there's no one else here just now, we're all meeting up later. Yeah, I'm fine. We're going out later. To the gig. I will. I promise, I will. Mum, . . . I love you. I'm FINE. OK, bye.

She hangs up and slumps.

Cork Woman *comes back.*

Young Woman   Did you have your cigarette?

Cork Woman   No, they sent us back. Made us feel like children.

English Woman *comes back in.*

English Woman   Jesus, you think we wanted to do a shit in their garden.

Young Woman *giggles. They ignore her.*

Cork Woman   Fuck it. Let's just smoke out the window.

Young Woman   But we'll get in trouble.

The other two women look at each other. They walk to the window and open it.

English Woman   I don't even smoke, but in the spirit of solidarity.

They light up. **English Woman** *coughs.*

English Woman   Your hair colour is pretty fab.

Cork Woman   Thanks. I do it myself.

English Woman   Oooh.

Young Woman (*trying to join in*)   Yeah, it's nice.

They ignore her.

English Woman   With what?

Cork Woman   Just Elvive.

English Woman   Really nice. You going to your mum's tomorrow?

Cork Woman   Yeah, just for the night.

English Woman (*laughs*)   Nuns. 'Cunts.'

Cork Woman   Oh, I know. My mum never had any truck with them. It really made her stand out when I was young. She was the only parent I knew who didn't even pretend to believe. My poor dad would religiously bring us to mass every Sunday and she'd just stay at home. It used to worry him but she wouldn't bend. She just thought they were hypocrites.

Young Woman   They've done some good too.

They look at each other and ignore her.

Cork Woman   Are you religious?

English Woman   Oh no, only in a vicarage, village fête kind of way.

Cork Woman   Would ye be dancing round the maypole?

English Woman   Not quite. Close enough though.

Cork Woman   They just seem all of a one to me. Village fêtes and maypoles.

English Woman   Don't you have fêtes?

Cork Woman   Not really.

Young Woman   We have sales of work.

They ignore her.

English Woman   Gosh, you're a very uncivilized lot.

Cork Woman   Careful now.

English Woman   Oh, I'm sorry, a very sensitive lot.

Young Woman (*loudly*)   You're being dicks.

Silence.

English Woman   Excuse me?

Young Woman   You are. It's really mean to sit there ignoring me. I know I upset you both and I'm sorry for that. I was just asking questions. I would have thought they'd be questions you'd have asked yourself. If you can't answer those questions without exploding at me, without getting defensive, well, that's on you. Maybe you're not quite as at ease with this as you're letting on.

Cork Woman   Who's at ease? Nobody's at ease here.

English Woman   I'm at ease. I just don't like being judged.

Young Woman   I wasn't judging you.

Cork Woman   It felt like it. And it's precisely because we have examined this decision before taking it, that it's painful to be quizzed on it.

Silence.

Young Woman   You said I was raped.

Cork Woman   You were.

Young Woman   That kind of thing happens ALL the time. I think it's happened to most of my friends.

Cork Woman   Maybe you all shouldn't drink so much.

Young Woman   Maybe.

English Woman   Or maybe she should be able to get as drunk as she wants without that happening.

Cork Woman   Yes. Maybe.

Young Woman   It was horrible. I can just remember bits. And the smell of him. It was fucking horrible. But DON'T say I was raped.

Cork Woman   Why?

Young Woman   Because I don't want that. I don't want to be a 'victim'. And what good is it? Like what am I gonna do with that exactly? Report it to the police? And have them ask me how much I drank? Have people go through my texts? Talk about my character? And for what? If it did go to court, to what, see people line up to shake his hand? To see him get a suspended sentence? And then what? To be *known* as that? Like to have people only see you that way. Connected to the worst thing that ever happened to you. To not be able to just move through the world as yourself but rather as a *victim*? So just don't say it. I'm gonna just move on and live my life exactly like most women do.

Cork Woman   Can you?

Young Woman   Yes . . . yes . . . But this . . . *this* is hard. Being here. I wish I hadn't had to. And I'm afraid that this will follow me. Do you know what I mean? I don't know how I feel? I mean I feel relieved, I think. I feel more like myself somehow but I feel sad too. I'm scared this will hurt me more. I'm afraid it *all* has hurt me. Damaged me. Ya know? I don't want my life coloured by all this. And the secrecy of it is just shite. Really shite. I only told my friend because I was in shock still when I met him but I really wish my mum was here. I wish I could tell my friends. I don't want this. Like what's next? What's my life gonna be like now?

Beat.

Cork Woman   It's your life, hon. It's up to you.

They all sit there for a bit.

English Woman   Men are fucking pigs.

Orderly *pokes his head around the door, big smile.*

Orderly   Ladies, anyone like a sneaky cup of tea? I'm heading off now but I thought I might as well drop you one before I go.

Cork Woman   Will it be as shite as your scrambled eggs?

Orderly   Well there's gratitude. And I brought some biscuits as well.

He begins doling out the tea and biscuits.

English Woman   Thanks, mate. You're not a fucking pig.

Orderly   Well I, I don't know what to say. Much obliged.

English Woman   You're welcome.

Orderly   Well girls, I'm off. I'll see you bright and early.

English Woman   You off out tonight?

Orderly   Nah mate, me and my man are sitting in and chilling.

Cork Woman   He's a lucky guy.

Orderly   You tell him that. I'm blue in the face telling him.

He looks out the window again.

Orderly   Hmm, I might have to get Mary to her bus first. She's still there. (*He shakes his head.*) Well, sleep tight, eh? (*He looks at them.*) Nearly there.

Cork Woman   Nearly there.

English Woman   Thanks.

Young Woman   Good night.

He leaves.

English Woman   Tea's shit.

Cork Woman   Mother of God, how is it possible to make such a shite cup of tea?

Young Woman   Brutal.

They sip anyway and munch on their biscuits.

Cork Woman   Pure shite, like.

Young Woman   Pure shite.

English Woman   Pure shite indeed.

Cork Woman   Let's go to sleep, shall we?

They all put their cups down.

They all move to their respective beds and lie down.

Silence.

There's the sound of a fart.

English Woman   Sorry 'bout that.

Giggles from all three beds.

Lights down.

Dreamlike video footage in transition.

Act Three

Morning.

Lights slowly up as if sun rising.

Chants of protest from outside.

Young Woman *is looking out the window.* **Cork Woman** *is brushing her hair.*

Orderly *enters.*

Orderly   Rise and shine, ladies. Breakfast's up

He begins passing out the trays. **English Woman** *groggily stirs.*

Orderly   Not too many out there today. You should be OK leaving.

Young Woman   Do you ever get hassle coming in and out?

Orderly   Oh my days. Do I get hassle? You know I get hassle.

Young Woman   Jasus.

Orderly   Jasus is right, my friend. When they give me hassle I walk in like this pass 'em.

He struts a little with his finger in the air.

Cork Woman   It's well for you is able to.

Orderly   They love me. Don't you think about them.

He walks to window and puts his finger up.

Young Woman *ducks.*

Orderly   You've got to man up, Queen.

Young Woman   Would ya stop?

He chuckles at her and then looks out the window again. His face drops a little.

Orderly   Hmmm. They're new.

He watches a little concerned for a moment.

English Woman   Mate, can I get a shower?

Orderly   Yeah, mate. Just outside on the left.

English Woman   Thanks.

He watches the crowd outside again for a beat, then turns back.

Orderly   Well Queens, top of the morning.

He bows and leaves.

Cork Woman   Fucking hell. Scrambled eggs again. He's got a bleeding cheek.

Young Woman   Boke.

Cork Woman   Well, drink your orange juice. We can't afford to get scurvy, eh?

They drink. **English Woman** *is still lying in bed.*

Cork Woman   You OK there?

English Woman   Oh, feeling a bit queasy.

Young Woman   I'll call someone.

English Woman   Nah, nah it's OK. It's what happens.

Young Woman   How do you know?

English Woman   I was like that before. The last time.

Young Woman*'s eyes widen but* **Cork Woman** *gives her a ferocious look.*

English Woman   I'll go have a shower.

She pulls on a dressing gown and tries to get up. She's not able.

Cork Woman *goes over to her and helps her to her feet.*

Cork Woman   Are you sure you shouldn't just lie down?

English Woman   No, I'll be OK. Thanks, I'll feel better once I have a shower.

Cork Woman *walks her to the door and she shuffles out.*

Young Woman   She's very pale.

Cork Woman   Yeah, well, let's keep an ear out.

They keep watching out and listening uncertainly for a moment.

Young Woman   When do you go back?

Cork Woman   Couple more days. I wish it was today. I miss my kids.

Young Woman   How many do you have again?

Cork Woman   Three. Ten, eight and six.

Young Woman   Nice.

Cork Woman   Yeah, they're great. They get on great. The older one really looks out for the other two. But the youngest bosses the older two around. Gas.

Young Woman   What's the middle one like?

Cork Woman   Oh, he's a dote. I mean they all are. But he's quite soft but reserved. A deep little thinker. The other two are ringers for their dad but he's more like me.

Young Woman   He looks like you?

Cork Woman   Well yeah, he does I suppose, but it's more than that. You know it's a very strange thing when you see your physical or personality traits showing up in these small people. It just lands on you again. I made that small person. Like he's got these real chubby thighs like me and his legs are slightly bow legged like mine. And then, he has all these little ways, like I'd do something, move my face in a certain way or react in a certain way and I'd realise it's something he does. And then I wonder, is he taking after me or am I taking after him you know. It's funny.

Young Woman   Ah.

Cork Woman   Oh now.

She looks like she might to cry.

Young Woman   Oh don't. Don't.

Cork Woman   It just takes it out of you. In ways you couldn't know. In ways nobody tells you. Like the guilt, it's just always there. You just live with it. Am I good enough? Have I damaged them by saying that or doing that or not saying or doing something? It's never ending. And I say this to you and it sounds awful but it's not, it's also the greatest thing that's ever happened to me. You know. Absolutely the greatest. It's just hard sometimes to be anything other than a mother. It all feels impossible sometimes.

Young Woman   But you're the best mum they could have. Like no one else could be better than you. You know?

Cork Woman   Hah.

Young Woman   It's true.

Cork Woman   I know that. Thanks, love. Thanks.

English Woman *comes back. She still looks very shaky.*

English Woman   Well, I feel a bit more human. You guys should have one.

Cork Woman   Nah, I just want to get out of here.

Young Woman   Me too.

But they don't move.

English Woman *gets to the bed and lies on top of the cover.*

Sounds of people on the streets outside.

Young Woman   What happens now?

No answer.

English Woman   Did you guys sleep alright?

Cork Woman   Ah.

Young Woman   Nah, had mad dreams.

English Woman   Don't tell us. Nothing more boring than someone's dreams.

Young Woman *smiles.*

Noise of protestors outside, less praying now, more shouts of 'Shame' etc.

Cork Woman   Jesus Christ.

She walks to the window.

Check this out.

Young Woman *walks to join her at the front of the stage and look out,* **English Woman** *follows slowly. They put their arms around each other,* **English Woman** *in the middle, they are supporting her gently.*

Young Woman   They're throwing eggs.

Cork Woman   Fuckers.

They watch for another moment.

Cork Woman   Well, c'mon amigas, it's time to step back into our lives.

English Woman   Through the madding crowd.

Young Woman   The madarse crowd.

The three turn away and stand for a moment with their arms still on each other's shoulders, and we see their little bums through the gaps in the hospital gowns.

English Woman   Let's get out of this purgatory.

They move to their beds, **Cork Woman** *and* **Young Woman** *dress in silence,* **English Woman** *lies down again.*

Young Woman   I don't even know your names.

Cork Woman   No.

English Woman   No.

Pause.

Young Woman   I'm Evelyn.

Beat.

Cork Woman (*to* **English Woman**)   Are you sure you're OK?

English Woman   Yeah, yeah.

Cork Woman *picks up her bag.*

Cork Woman   Well, goodbye. Good luck.

English Woman   Bye, enjoy the shopping

Cork Woman   Thanks.

Young Woman   Bye. Enjoy your homecoming.

Cork Woman   Oh, I will.

She leaves. She comes straight back in and walks to **English Woman**.

Cork Woman   I don't think you're OK.

English Woman   I think I've started bleeding again.

Cork Woman *looks.*

Cork Woman   I'm gonna call someone.

She runs out. **Young Woman** *walks to* **English Woman**'s *bed.*

English Woman   I'm cold. Are you?

Young Woman   No. I'm not.

Young Woman *runs to her bed and gets the cover, runs back and puts it on top of* **English Woman**. *She rubs her back.*

Cork Woman *and* **Orderly** *come back in.*

Orderly   What's up with my friend?

Young Woman   She's shivering.

Orderly (*to* **English Woman**)   You alright, mate? We get you out to the doctor, shall we? Can you walk? No?

He walks around and unclicks the wheels of the bed.

Young Woman   Is she alright?

Orderly   We'll make sure she is.

English Woman   Ooooohhhh, mate no, I wanna go home. I have to go to work /

Orderly   / Soon, soon.

English Woman   Please, please I'll be fine, please.

Orderly   Sorry mate, better safe than sorry.

He wheels her out. **Cork Woman** *and* **Young Woman** *stand looking at each other.*

Young Woman   Should we wait?

Cork Woman   Nah, I dunno . . . Nah . . . Maybe a few minutes.

They sit down on their beds.

Cork Woman   Will you get to see much of London?

Young Woman   Oh. I don't know. I don't think so. We haven't a bean.

Cork Woman   Well, London Fields is nice and strolling about Hackney there. Or Hampstead is worth a visit. There's lots to do with no money. Well, not lots but you know.

Young Woman   Thanks.

They look towards the door.

Cork Woman   And when you get home, maybe you should think about talking to someone. About what happened to you. You owe it to your future self. Give yourself a chance.

Young Woman   Oh. OK.

Orderly *comes back in.*

Cork Woman   Is she OK?

Orderly   She'll be OK.

They look at him uncertainly.

Orderly   She will be.

Young Woman   Should we wait?

Orderly   Aw no, I don't think she'll be going home today, but you guys are all good to go.

Cork Woman   OK, thanks.

Orderly   Mind yourselves now, ladies. Till the next time.

They look at him hard.

Orderly   I mean . . . See ya.

He goes to leave then turns.

Orderly   And remember. Hold your heads up going out.

They nod. He nods back at them. He leaves.

Cork Woman   Right, Well, I am going this time.

Young Woman   OK, I'm just waiting for my friend.

Cork Woman   Do go and talk to someone. I mean it. You have to take care of yourself. We all have to. Take care of ourselves.

Young Woman *nods.* **Cork Woman** *leaves with a little wave.*

Young Woman *sits on her bed for a bit. Then she pulls out her phone and dials.*

Young Woman   Mum, hey. Oh, I just wanted to give you a call. It was good, yeah. (*Beat, decides.*) Oh well, actually, not really. I'm not really having a great time. No, I'm fine. I am fine. I'll tell you when I see you. No, when I see you. I will, I promise. I'm just a little . . . sad. But I will tell you. I'll see

you tomorrow and we can have a chat then. I'm fine. Mum,
I love you. You're the best. OK, see you tomorrow. I'm
FINE. I am. I will tell you . . . I'll be fine.

*She sits on the bed for a moment then she walks to the front and looks
out the window again, out front. She looks at the audience.*

She sits on the bed again.

Young Man *enters. His jacket is covered in egg yolks.*

Young Man   Hello.

Young Woman   Hello. (*She notices the eggs on his jacket.*) Oh,
They got you.

Young Man   Ah. How you feeling?

Young Woman   Yeah fine, thanks. Did you have a good
night?

Young Man   Yeah, it was really fun. Everyone was asking
for you. I told them you were visiting family.

Young Woman   OK.

Young Man   How was your night?

She looks at him.

Young Man   Good?

Young Woman   No, no it wasn't at all.

Young Man   No doubt . . . Let's get out of here. There's an
emergency exit, we can get out and avoid any nonsense.

Young Woman   No. We'll just go out the front.

Young Man   Really?

Young Woman   Yeah. (*She walks towards the window and looks
out.*) Fuck them.

Young Man   OK.

Young Woman *starts to gather her things.* **Young Man** *takes off his jacket.*

She picks up the glass paraffin lamp he bought her.

Young Woman   This is lovely.

Young Man   Ah. A souvenir.

She puts it her bag. He cringes at what he said.

Young Woman   What's the plan tonight?

Young Man   Well, there's another gig, you probably won't want to go and that's fine but /

Young Woman   / No, we'll go.

Young Man   Are you sure?

Young Woman   Yeah, I'll go. It'll be good. (*She smiles at him.*) I'm absolutely sure.

As they walk out he puts his jacket around her shoulders.

Noises off of protests.

Fast play of video images and soundscape of streets, people, life builds to blackout.

End of Play.

Discover. Read. Listen. Watch.

A NEW WAY TO ENGAGE WITH PLAYS

This award-winning digital library features over 3,000 playtexts, 400 audio plays, 300 hours of video and 360 scholarly books.

Playtexts published by Methuen Drama, The Arden Shakespeare, Faber & Faber, Playwrights Canada Press, Aurora Metro Books and Nick Hern Books.

Audio Plays from L.A. Theatre Works featuring classic and modern works from the oeuvres of leading American playwrights.

Video collections including films of live performances from the RSC, The Globe and The National Theatre, as well as acting masterclasses and BBC feature films and documentaries.

Methuen Drama Modern Plays

include

Bola Agbaje
Edward Albee
Ayad Akhtar
Jean Anouilh
John Arden
Peter Barnes
Sebastian Barry
Clare Barron
Alistair Beaton
Brendan Behan
Edward Bond
William Boyd
Bertolt Brecht
Howard Brenton
Amelia Bullmore
Anthony Burgess
Leo Butler
Jim Cartwright
Lolita Chakrabarti
Caryl Churchill
Lucinda Coxon
Tim Crouch
Shelagh Delaney
Ishy Din
Claire Dowie
David Edgar
David Eldridge
Dario Fo
Michael Frayn
John Godber
James Graham
David Greig
John Guare
Lauren Gunderson
Peter Handke
David Harrower
Jonathan Harvey
Robert Holman
David Ireland
Sarah Kane

Barrie Keeffe
Jasmine Lee-Jones
Anders Lustgarten
Duncan Macmillan
David Mamet
Patrick Marber
Martin McDonagh
Arthur Miller
Alistair McDowall
Tom Murphy
Phyllis Nagy
Anthony Neilson
Peter Nichols
Ben Okri
Joe Orton
Vinay Patel
Joe Penhall
Luigi Pirandello
Stephen Poliakoff
Lucy Prebble
Peter Quilter
Mark Ravenhill
Philip Ridley
Willy Russell
Jackie Sibblies Drury
Sam Shepard
Martin Sherman
Chris Shinn
Wole Soyinka
Simon Stephens
Kae Tempest
Anne Washburn
Laura Wade
Theatre Workshop
Timberlake Wertenbaker
Roy Williams
Snoo Wilson
Frances Ya-Chu Cowhig
Benjamin Zephaniah

For a complete listing of
Methuen Drama titles, visit:
www.bloomsbury.com/drama

Follow us on Twitter and keep up to date
with our news and publications
@MethuenDrama